Cowboy Logic

The Wit & Wisdom of the West

Rounded up by Ted Stone

Red Deer College Press

The Publishers
Red Deer College Press, 56 Avenue & 32 Street Box
5005, Red Deer Alberta Canada T4N 5H5

Acknowledgements
Cover design by Kurt Hafso. Text design by Dennis
Johnson. Printed and bound in Canada by Parkland
ColourPress for Red Deer College Press.

Financial support provided by the Alberta
Foundation for the Arts, a beneficiary of the Lottery
Fund of the Government of Alberta, and by the
Canada Council, the Department of Canadian
Heritage and Red Deer College.

COMMITTED TO THE DEVELOPMENT OF CULTURE AND THE ARTS

5 4 3 2 1

Canadian Cataloguing in Publication Data

Cowboy logic

(Roundup books)
ISBN 0-88995-152-7

1. Cowboys—Canada, Western—Humor. 2. Ranch life—
Canada, Western—Humor. 3. Cowboys—Canada,
Western—Quotations, maxims, etc. 4. Ranch life—
Canada, Western—Quotations, maxims, etc.5. Canadian
wit and humor (English) I. Stone, Ted, 1947– II. Series:
Roundup books (Red Deer, Alta.)
PS8375.C69 1996   C818'.540208'092636   C95-911207-3
PR9197.8.C69 1996

Editor's Note
The quotations in this book come after two
decades gathering the words and stories of
Western people.

~1~

Never cry over spilt milk—it could have been whisky.

~2~

Getting old ain't so bad when you consider the alternative.

~3~

If it ain't broke, don't fix it.

~4~

Never wrestle with a pig. You both get dirty and the pig likes it.

~5~

Whenever a job's hard, you're doing it wrong.

~6~

There's only one way to look at a politician
—down.

~7~

90% of the politi-cians give the rest of them a bad name.

~8~

The only thing you
get out of life is
what you eat.

It's better to keep your mouth shut and have people think you're an idiot than speak up and have them know it.

~10~

Never go to bed mad.
Stay up and fight.

~11~

Y ou live and learn,
but then you die
and forget.

~12~

It's hard to put a foot in a closed mouth.

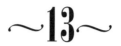

~13~

The meek shall inherit the earth—but they won't get the grazing rights.

~14~

If you don't go to bed tired, you didn't get up early enough or work hard enough.

People who aren't sleepy when they go to bed usually are when they wake up.

~16~

A man can get whipped, but that don't mean he's beat.

~17~

If you can't afford what you want, want what you got.

~18~

Never spoil a good story by sticking to the facts. It's hardly worth talkin' if you're going to tell the truth.

~19~

Almost anything is easier to get into than out of.

~20~

Y ou don't have to go to law school to know how to tell the truth, but it helps if you're planning to lie.

~21~

There's no such thing
as strong coffee—
only weak people.

~22~

Asking a dumb question is easier than fixing a dumb mistake.

~23~

The only good thing
you can say about
tight boots is that they'll
make you forget your
other troubles.

~24~

Love is like the morning dew—it's as likely to settle on a cow chip as a flower.

～25～

Promises don't butter bread.

~26~

Everything is
interesting if you
know enough about it.

~27~

You can't tell what
way the train went
by looking at the railroad
tracks.

~28~

People who brag about their ancestors are like turnips—the best part of 'em is buried.

~29~

Every jackass thinks he has horse sense.

~30~

Good things come to those who wait and work to beat hell while they're waitin'.

~31~

It's better when people wonder why you didn't say something than why you did.

~32~

The surest way to predict cold weather is to wait until the stock tank freezes.

~33~

Politicians never lie, unless it's absolutely convenient.

~34~

Take care of your pennies and your dollars will take care of themselves.

~35~

Everything evens out in the end. In the old days, the buffalo were almost killed off. Now we've got all we need and the railroads are going extinct.

~36~

The best things in life
are free, but it
usually takes money to
appreciate 'em.

~37~

Anything you do, do with all your might, because anything worth doin' is worth doin' right.

~38~

Never trust anyone
who thinks he knows
what's best for everyone
else.

~39~

Always be in a hurry to lend a hand, but slow to ask for one.

~40~

Money can buy you a dog, but it can't make him wag his tail.

~41~

Never miss a chance to mind your own business.

~42~

There's no accounting for luck, but it's generally true that the harder you work the luckier you get.

~43~

No matter what
anybody tells you,
nothing is ever free.

~44~

Have trust in your fellow man, but be sure to brand your calves.

~45~

You'll never get ahead following the crowd.

~46~

Sometimes, it's better to ask for forgiveness than permission.

~47~

When opportunity knocks somebody has to be home to answer the door.

~48~

It's almost always better
not to do what
everyone else is doing.

~49~

The best things to eat
come in a pie.

~50~

The surest way to keep
a secret is to forget it.

~51~

The wise don't learn
from their mistakes.
They learn from other
people's mistakes.

~52~

Never say anything bad about somebody who isn't there. You might be talking to a relative.

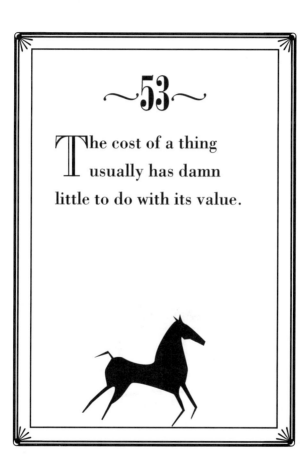

~53~

The cost of a thing
usually has damn
little to do with its value.

~54~

Never piss into the wind or drink downstream from the cattle.

~55~

In the cattle business,
look out for anybody
who has to bring a lawyer
with him to talk a deal.

~56~

Never put all your eggs in one basket—
unless they're already cooked.

~57~

When you wake up, get up. When you get up, stay up.

A little learning is a
dangerous thing, but
a lot of ignorance is a
whole bunch worse.

~59~

There's nothing more questionable than an expert's opinion—unless it's two experts' opinions.

~**60**~

A rancher should always live within his income, even when he has to borrow money to do it.

~61~

Y̶ou have to believe in luck. How else can you explain some people's success.

~62~

It don't matter how much somebody talks, just so long as they do it in the fewest possible words.

~63~

Facts are like cattle breeds—everybody's got their own opinion on 'em.

~64~

A banker is somebody who'll lend you money if you can prove to him that you don't need it.

~65~

These days, common
sense ain't as
common as it used to be.

~66~

Experience might be the best teacher, but the costs of that kind of schooling run awful high.

BACK to School

~**67**~

A pet lamb makes a cross ram.

~68~

You might not be able to get blood from a turnip, but you can usually get the turnip.

~69~

The trouble with people who grow up in town is that most of them never learn how to do anything.

~70~

A good horse goes until he can't go anymore, and then he goes some more.

~71~

Whenever you stand still, you're losing ground.

~72~

It's hard for people to argue with what you don't say.

~73~

Some people never come in out of the rain until after the storm's over.

~74~

Good intentions don't saddle-break an ornery horse.

~75~

Anybody who marries for money will end up paying for it.

~76~

Some people spend more time wantin' what they don't have than enjoying what they do.

~77~

Income tax has caused more ranchers to go out of business than low cattle prices. Before there was income tax nobody kept track of how bad things really were.

~78~

It doesn't do any good to close the barn door after the horses get out, but you might just as well.

~79~

Never get dressed up to impress people. Anybody who knows you won't be impressed, and anybody who don't know you won't notice.

~80~

Some people exaggerate
so much they can't tell
the truth without lying.

~81~

The trouble with national elections is that anybody fit for office won't run and anybody who'll run ain't fit.

~82~

Never trust big talk.
Empty wagons
always do the most
rattling.

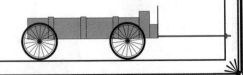

~83~

The only weather prediction that'll hold true in a dry spell is that a drought always ends with a rain.

~84~

Make the most of yourself. It's all there is of you.

~85~

If you want to be successful in life, find something you like to do that makes money, then get really good at it. If what you like to do is raise cattle, get really good at something else, too.

~86~

It's better to wear out
than rust out.

~87~

Some people are so
open-minded their
brains appear to have
spilled out the hole.

~88~

No matter how low the value of a dollar falls, there'll always be somebody around who'll stoop low enough to get it.

~89~

Big talk ain't worth much on a bull ride.

~**90**~

Money won't buy happiness, but it can make unhappiness sorta comfortable.

~91~

Knowledge is a good thing. The trouble is some people know a whole lot that ain't true.

~92~

Always be humble. If you're humble, you'll be thankful, and if you're thankful, you'll be happy.

~93~

Some people mistake
imagination for
memory, and luck for
good sense.

~94~

An expert is some-body who wears a suit and comes from at least fifty miles away.

~95~

Nobody's so poor they can't keep a horse. A lot of people are so poor they'll keep several.

~96~

Whatever you need to get, make sure you get it got.

~97~

It's good to give people a hand when they need it, but sooner or later everybody has to saddle his own horse.

~98~

It don't matter how big a ranch you own, or how many cows you brand, or how much money you make, the size of your funeral is still going to depend on the weather.

~99~

You can tell more about a man's character from the way he treats his stock than the church he belongs to.

~100~

The best time to hold your tongue is when you feel like you have the most to say.

~101~

If you run a ranch, look out for small expenses. A little leak will sink a great ship.

～102～

Whenever you have to choose the lesser of two evils, you should always keep in mind that you're still choosing evil.

~103~

Never take a bull by the horns. Take him by the tail. That way you can let go.

~104~

Breakfast is the most important meal of the day. If you don't get home in time for breakfast, you're liable to be in real trouble.

~105~

Never trade horses in the middle of a stream.

~106~

Some cattlemen are accused of being land greedy when all they're really after is whatever little bit of property happens to border their ranch.

~107~

Never put up with anything that doesn't work right.

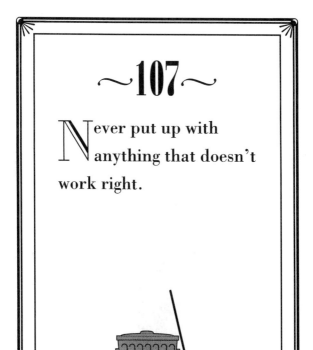

~108~

Experience makes some men wise, and others afraid.

~109~

Pray for an easy winter, but put up lots of hay.

~110~

It don't matter how tall your grandfather was—you still have to do your own growing.

~111~

The problem with just doing things good enough is that most of the time good enough ain't good enough.

~112~

A man should count himself lucky if he can look back on his life and say that he has had at least one great horse, one exceptional dog, and one true friend.

~113~

In the end, everybody's equal. While you're alive, there'll always be somebody richer, stronger and smarter than you. But once you're dead, nobody will ever be deader.

~114~

It doesn't cost anything to smile, and even if it did it would be worth the price.

~115~

Never give people
advice unless you
know the kind they'd
like to follow.

~116~

There's no use having an itch if you can't scratch it.

~117~

Never get mad about anything you can do something about—or anything you can't do something about.

~118~

The proof of success ain't necessary.

~119~

Be sure you're right, then go ahead.

~120~

Just think how much sadder a place the world would be if you didn't have yourself to laugh at.

~121~

Nothing is as good as it used to be, including your memory.

~122~

Never be in a hurry
until you're sure of
where you're going.

~123~

Some people envy the rich, but they ought to remember that a fattened steer ain't so lucky.

~124~

Will Rogers had it right when he said to always live your life so that whenever you lose, you're ahead. Just get a few laughs and do the best you can.